By Jan Glaesel

The Complete Method For Trumpet

IMPROVE YOUR GAME

WARM-UPS - INTERVAL & SLURRING EXERCISES

Volume I

WRITTEN BY: JAN GLAESEL
COPYRIGHT © 2012:
JAN GLAESEL / JGMUSIK APS DK
WWW.TRUMPETGAME.COM

INDEX - VOLUME I

COLOPHONE: TITEL: IMPROVE YOUR GAME - VOLUME I - 1. EDITION · AUTHOR: JAN GLAESEL · PUBLISHER & COPYRIGHT: JGMUSIK APS · DK 2012 · ISBN: ISBN 978-87-92945-00-6 · LAYOUT: AJOUR GRAFISK DESIGN · COVERPHOTO: HANS OLE MADSEN · WEBSITE: WWW.TRUMPETGAME.COM · CONTACT: INFO@TRUMPETGAME.COM

FOREWORD:

This is actually the second time I'm writing this foreword. Right now I'm sitting at Starbucks in Central Pattaya, Thailand. I've just spent the last two weeks here in solitude in this wonderful country, away from home, work, phones and daily decisions, to finally finish my Trumpet Method Book "Improve Your Game – The Complete Method Book for Trumpet"

This project started in 2004, and the first time I wrote this foreword was in 2008 somewhere in the airspace between the U.S. and Denmark. I had been working in Las Vegas as a musical director for one of my Danish friends, a musical show genius, who wanted to try things out "over there". In my spare time, I collected all my notes on practising into one huge pile, and then thought, "That's it – the book is done". But boy was I wrong. When I got back home, I started looking at my "new book" – and it was a complete mess. It took me another four years to complete this project, inventing new systems and exercises to make the project come together. Now I have a complete overview of my material, have tried most of my ideas on myself, and now feel confident knowing that I have something of real value to pass on to my fellow trumpet players.

HERE IS MY STORY:

While playing drums at the age of 6 in the Tivoli Boys Guard in Copenhagen, I practised the trumpet, and 8 years old I got my spot in the marching band and just fell in love with the instrument. I spent 10 years in Tivoli and by the time I retired at 16 years of age, I was a semi-professional musician. I could sight-read music, follow a conductor, learned to be on time, and learned all of the other things that make you successful in the business. But suddenly, I was "unemployed".

In high school I joined some different bands playing all different kinds of music. In the beginning I had a huge problem: There was no music to read!!! My whole life I had played from written music, and now suddenly I had to just play something and improvise. I was completely lost for a while, but with time came the courage to jump without a parachute. It sounded awful, and other trumpet players would probably have been kicked out of the band (unless you had a van or a rehearsal room), but I had something else. Due to my training in The Tivoli

Boys Guard, I had the power and technique to play all the high stuff, and I could play for hours without getting tired. On top of that I knew my theory, and had a flair for composing and arranging. So, whenever somebody needed an arrangement or song – they knew who to call. I stayed in business and started getting a lot of work. In 1979 I had the fortune to be approached by the Big Band Guru Thad Jones, who at that time lived in Denmark wanted to form a Danish/American big band - Eclipse. For the next 3 years I learned everything about being a big band section-player. That was an experience of a lifetime.

To cut a long story short, I ended up as Musical Director on Danish National TV and was placed in charge of some of the biggest acts in the entertainment business in Denmark. I became known as the guy who could play trumpet with one hand, and conduct with the other – and actually I can. I formed my own company writing music for feature film and commercials – boy I've written a lot of those.

A day is only 24 hours – that's a fact. So with a schedule as busy as mine has been for the last 20 years, I of course had to cut some corners. Since practising didn't pay bills, and wasn't fun – I cut down on that. For many years I never practised. I just played, played and played, because I didn't have the time to invest.

THIS WAS THE WAY IT USED TO BE

After months of preparation, writing, rehearsing and just minutes before the first downbeat on the opening night of a show, I would ask the band: "Has anybody seen my horn?" I would find it, oil the valves and just give it a kick in the #¤%&, and would (barely) survive that first night. After a couple of shows it would get easier, and no one would suspect that I never practiced. The truth of the matter was that if you had given me a simple Danish Folksong and asked me to play it mezzopiano – I would have tanked completely.

THE CROSSROAD

By 2004, we had played thousands of shows during a 15 year period so we decided to take an indefinite break. This wasn't a big problem for me as I had all my writing, arranging and producing jobs. BUT – what about my beloved trumpet? Now I had two options:

SELL MY HORNS - OR - START TO PRACTICE!!

This book is the proof of my decision. The way back to falling in love with my instrument again has been long, frustrating, and hard, but above all – really, really rewarding.

THE FIRST DAY AT "WORK"

After making the decision to find out how good a trumpet player I could have been, I started to practice. I had promised myself to practice at least one hour a day, and that sounded within reach for me. Then I experienced the scariest moment in my professional life. I went to my studio, got out the trumpet and stared at it for a loooong time, not knowing what to play. I played some scales – enough to make an hour pass by. But when I looked at the clock, only 3 minutes had passed. I put down the horn, and gave up.

I've never been good at defeat, so the next day I found my very old copy of Arban's Complete Conservatory Method For Trumpet. The Arban had been the bible for me in the Tivoli Boys Guard. I knew my way around it, but it had been a long time since I looked at it. I put together a one hour program of exercises from the Arban book, and had a really hard time getting it together. On the negative side it soon occurred to me what a lousy technique I had, but on the positive side, I started to improve – fast. Nothing is more rewarding than when you put in the effort and start getting results.

At a lecture in Copenhagen, American Business Coach **Keith Cunningham** came with a statement that really was an eye-opener for me. He said:

"IF YOU HAVE A TALENT, NO MATTER WHAT IT IS, AND SPEND 3 HOURS A DAY FOR 3 YEARS ON IMPROVING YOUR SKILLS, YOU WILL AFTER THOSE 3 YEARS BE IN THE TOP 100 IN YOUR FIELD - WORLDWIDE!!"

An average lifespan is roughly 700,000 hours and you only have to spend 3,285 hours of those to get in the top 100 worldwide. How easy is that!! OK – if you want to stay at the top 100 or get to #1, you have to put in a lot of additional hours – but you get the picture.

Since I restarted my practice career, I've studied a lot of books from great brass players, including Allen Vizzutti, Arturo Sandoval, Schlossberg, Clark, Herring, Stamp, Caruso, Claude Gordon – you name it. I also picked a lot of brains, met and played with some terrific trumpet players to get the material together that helped point me in the right direction, and I really want to share this research and material with you.

Let me get one thing straight:
I CAN'T PLAY EVERYTHING I WROTE IN THIS BOOK!!!!

If I only wrote exercises that I could play – I wouldn't learn anything. But I'm getting there: hour by hour, day by day, exercise by exercise. The day I can play everything in this book, I will write another. Here is a promise to you. If you can play the "Lyrical Interval Etude" that I wrote and dedicated to Mr. Malcolm McNab (in Vol. 4) I'll write a new one dedicated to you. (I can't play it – yet)

At age 54 I'm all fired up about playing and practicing my horn and I'm planning on improving my game for the next many years. I can't tell you when I'll stop – and as long as the horn sounds a little bit better every day I pick it up – I'll keep blowing.

JAN GLAESEL
Copenhagen, Denmark - 2012

HOW TO USE THIS BOOK

This book has been divided into 4 separate and independent volumes so that you can dig into specific areas instead of having to buy one large book just for one section, such as "The 10 Daily Routines" or "All Scales".

- **Vol. I – Warm-ups, interval & Slurring Exercises**
- **Vol. II – Pedal-tones & Low Notes / The 10 Daily Routines**
- **Vol. III – All Scales / Transposition & Dexterity Studies**
- **Vol. IV – Tonguing / Target, Precision & Endurance /Performance / Melodies & Etudes**

IMPORTANT!!

I've come up with three basic "rules" that apply to this book. They are:

1.   REST ALMOST AS MUCH AS YOU PLAY

Practising can be harder than playing a gig. When I started this journey, I would practise one hour a day. My mistake was that I played for a full hour without resting at all. So when 60 minutes were up, I was done, and after a couple of weeks my lips were like two bricks. If you want to practice playing your horn for one hour – you should practice for two hours. Get the idea? Rest is important.

2.   3 STRIKES AND YOU'RE OUT!!

This needs explanation. When you look through the book you will probably be a little intimidated over all the high notes and tiring phrases – don't be. All exercises are written so that every trumpet player on an intermediate level can benefit from them – as long as they practice using this **"3 strikes and you're out"** rule.

Whenever you reach your current range limit – **give it three attempts, then stop.** The next day you can give it a shot again. In a few days, you will experience that what was once impossible, is now a walk in the park.

Exercises like this are divided into two or three sections. If I state, "Don't continue beyond this point if not within your range", stay within you range a couple of more days, and it will come. Remember: **"Good Things Come To Those Who Wait."** And HEY!! If the whole high note concept isn't something interesting to you, don't go there!! Simply skip those exercises, and let your normal high C be the top of your range. Remember:
"No note is so high, that it can't be played an octave or two down"!!

3. PUT AS MUCH MUSIC AS POSSIBLE INTO EVERYTHING YOU PLAY

Let's face it – 95% of these exercises are plain boring when you just look at them. But if you try to put as much music or feeling into them when playing, you can make them come to life. On top of that you should play everything with the most beautiful sound you can imagine. These two things together are essential for getting to the point where time just flies when you practice.

In the Chapter on **Performance in Vol. 4**, I will share with you hundreds of ideas that made sense to me about trumpet playing that I picked up around fellow trumpet players and the internet. I call this, "Spiritual Tapas". In this same section, a good friend and fellow trumpet player **Jon Gorrie** will give you an introduction to his book "Performing In The Zone" – a book all performers should read.

LAST RULES:
"TREAT YOURSELF TO SOME OF THE ETUDES IN THE BACK OF EACH VOLUME"
&
"TAKE A DAY OFF FROM TRUMPET PLAYING EVERY WEEK!!"
LET'S PRACTICE!!

INTRODUCTION TO SELECTED STUDIES VOLUME 1

UNIVERSAL WARM UP - MY PERSONAL PG.13 - 19

A good warm up is essential for all trumpet players. I know that it's boring, but once you get into the habit you'll get the hang of it. A good warm-up will set you back 25 to 30 minutes in most method books. In my universe that's too much. 10 - 15 minutes is enough for me to soften up my lips.

A good warm up is necessary, but don't get too dependent on it. You should always be able to pick up your horn and start playing. Believe me, in the real world you will have to be able to do exactly that.

EXERCISE 1 PG. 13

Purely to soften up your lips and to get the air flowing. The tempo is only for guidance. You should time it so you're completely empty of air after each phrase.

EXERCISE 2 - 5 PG. 13 - 19

This will open up your sound and tune in your tongue. When you understand the principle of the exercise, close the book and play it by heart. Not reading will change your focus to the result. Finish of with the cool down phrase and take a 10 minute break before continuing.

ALTERNATIVE WARM UP. PG. 29 - 33

EXERCISE 1-2 PG. 29 - 30.

These exercises are related. Exercise 2 is a mirrored version of exercise 1.
Each exercise should be played with a full sound. When you understand the principle, close the book and just play it. Use your brain and ears.

EXERCISE 3 INTERVAL CADENZA PG. 31 - 33

This exercise is written to start airflow. It's builds around a standard I-IV-V7 progression. Again, once you understand the exercise, close the book and just play. Once you think you've got it all down, set yourself back by playing the suggested articulations.

EXERCISE 4 SCALE-SINGING PG. 34 - 35

If your horn sounds and feels clogged, scale-singing will solve the problem. This exercise takes you to standard high C. All trumpet players should have that within their range.

EXERCISE 5-6 WIDER SCALE-SINGING PG. 36 - 37

Here it's very important to implement the idea of "3 strikes and you're out". Playing all the way through the exercise will take you up to G above high C. Play until you reach your limit. Give it 3 attempts and then STOP!!!!!
The next day, play from the beginning again and see you can pass that your previous limit. If you continue with this I promise you that you'll expand you register to where you want. Play a cool down phrase where ever you stop.

THE LIP BENDER WARM UP PG. 38 - 39
EXERCISE 1

The lip bender warm up gives you a lot of control and is very good for intonation. Play the same phrase twice: first time with the correct fingering, and secondly by just bending the notes with the lips. The exercise follows the circle of fifths so you change intervals all the time.

EXERCISE 2

Don't play this exercise until you have mastered exercise 1

FLEXI WARM UP PG. 40 - 44
EXERCISE 1 PG. 40

Your focus should be on the interval between the first two notes in this exercise. Try to make the transition between the two notes (an ascending octave) as clean as possible by avoiding small tones or clicks in between notes.

EXERCISE 2 PG. 40

The same thing, but mirrored.

EXERCISE 3 PG. 40

The same as exercise 1 but ascending. The last two staves should be played using the "3 strikes and you're out" principle.

EXERCISE 4 PG. 41

The same thing, but mirrored.

EXERCISE 5 - 8 PG. 42 - 44

Same principle with clean switches between notes. Breathe every four bars, and use the "3 strikes and you're out" regime . This is important. Play the cool down phrase after you finish.

LEGATO POWER WARM-UP PG. 45 - 47
EXERCISE 1 PG. 45

This is one of the exercises I would bring to a desert island. If you use this exercise correctly, it will improve both your sound and range. Don't overdo. Use the "3 strikes..." concept. Play the cool down variations of the exercise on pg. 47 when after you've finished.

DANISH FOLKSONG PG. 48

This should be the final touch to every warm up you play, whether it's long or short. I suggest you play the Danish folk song "I skovens dybe stille ro" but you can choose other tunes if you like, such as "Yesterday" by the Beatles or "Fjariln vingad syns på Haga" (Swedish folksong) Find some of your own. Play it in 3 keys: C - F - Bb, and take a 30 second break in between. Play with a full sound and play the melody exactly as written - no valve-tricks to make up for the difficult intervals. Take a ten minute break before continuing.

INTERVAL STUDIES - MAJOR, MINOR & AUGMENTED EX 1-4 PG. 50 - 59

This exercise is quite simple and in four variations. Major, minor, augmented and a combo version. Please don't read it every time. Get the idea of the first couple of keys, and then think the rest. In that way you can focus a lot more on the purpose of the exercise. Please play with suggested dynamics to put as much music into the exercise as possible. Also play the suggested articulations for variation.

EXPANDING FLEXIBILITY-SLUR STUDIES EX. 1-7 PG. 60 - 69

These exercises are actually the same - the time just changes. Please use the directions for where to stop so that you don't overdo it. Focus on hitting the centre of pitch. Remember the "3 strikes and you're out" rule. It applies here more than anywhere. Do not continue with ex. 2 until you have mastered ex. 1 and so on.

ARBAN INSPIRED SLUR/FLEX STUDY EX. 6 -7 PG. 70 - 72

Try hitting the centre of the pitch in all intervals, and put as much music into the exercise as possible.

INTERVAL RANGE STUDY EX. 8 PG. 73

Focus on the expanding intervals and try to be precise. It's ok to slow down as the expansion increases, in order to get it right. Better safe than sorry. "3 strikes and you're out" applies here, so don't force it.

INTRODUCTION TO OCTAVE STUDIES AND OCTAVE STUDIES PG 78 - 81.

Read directions on page 78

OCTAVE LEGATO STUDY PG. 82

This exercise is filled with music. Focus on the octave jumps and play with a full open sound and have a constant air flow.

TREAT YOURSELF WITH SOME OF THE MUSICAL ETUDES & STUDIES PG. 86 - 95

LET'S GET GOING - AND REMEMBER THESE WISE WORDS:

"EVERYBODY WANTS TO BE THE HERO BUT NO ONE WANTS TO SLAY THE DRAGON"
QUOTE: WYNTON MARSALIS

My Personal

Universal Warm-Up

Please read "Introduction To Chapters" for reference - see index

14

Conclusion

Minor

3

mf

(Legato)   (Staccato)

Simile.........

Conclusion

4 Augmented

mf

Simile........

Conclusion

16

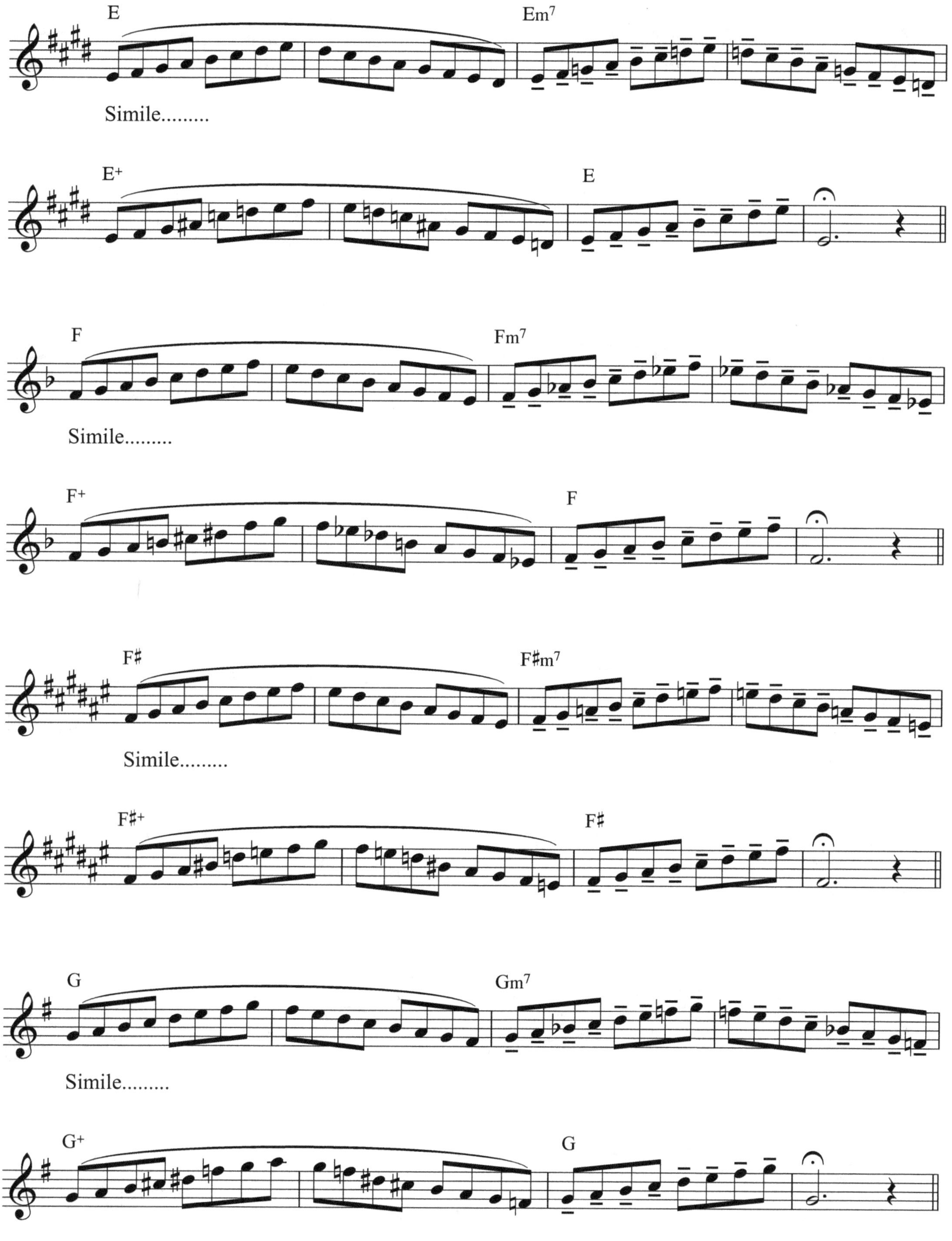
E
Em7
Simile.........
E+
E
F
Fm7
Simile.........
F+
F
F♯
F♯m7
Simile.........
F♯+
F♯
G
Gm7
Simile.........
G+
G

18

C

Cm⁷

Simile.........

C+

C

Cool down phrase

f

8vb

Take a 10 mininute break

This warm up covers all areas

The Gorrie Warm Up

Finishing this book I met with my good friend, trumpet player and author of the book "Performing in the Zone" Jon Gorrie, and we played together for a couple of days in Gothenburg where he lives. I surgested that we played his warm up routine - getting a new warm up routine, once in a while is very inspiring.

The good thing about Jon warm-up is that it forces you to get your breathing going, and also covers the pedaltone area. If you're not familiar with pedaltones, please go to the pedaltone chapter in Vol II first. Every four bars should be palyed in one breath. If you don't fill up your lungs, you'll be screwed the lover you get.

Here is Jon's personal touch to the start of every key - so your starting point is the same.

G Gm G° G
8vb
F♯ F♯m F♯° F♯
8vb
F Fm F° F
8vb
E Em E° E
8vb
E♭ E♭m E♭° E♭
8vb
D Dm D° D
8vb
D♭ D♭m D♭° D♭
8vb
C Cm C° C
8vb

Does everything work ? - Warm Up

On a regular basis, when time allows it, I meet with my good friend Nikolaj Viltoft, trumpetplayer at The Danish Royal Philharmonic, and we play for a couple of hours, drink coffee and finish of with a good lunch. We always exchange ideas, and last time he gave me this warm-up that kind of gives you a complete check-up on breathing and attack. The best aspect of this is that you mirror the exercise all the time - that forces you to stay focused.

I urge you to meet with fellow trumpet player once in a while to exchange ideas - it's so inspiring to find out, that what's hard for you, is exactly as hard for everybody else. Some times you feel that you're the only one with the problem. Guess what - You're NOT!!!

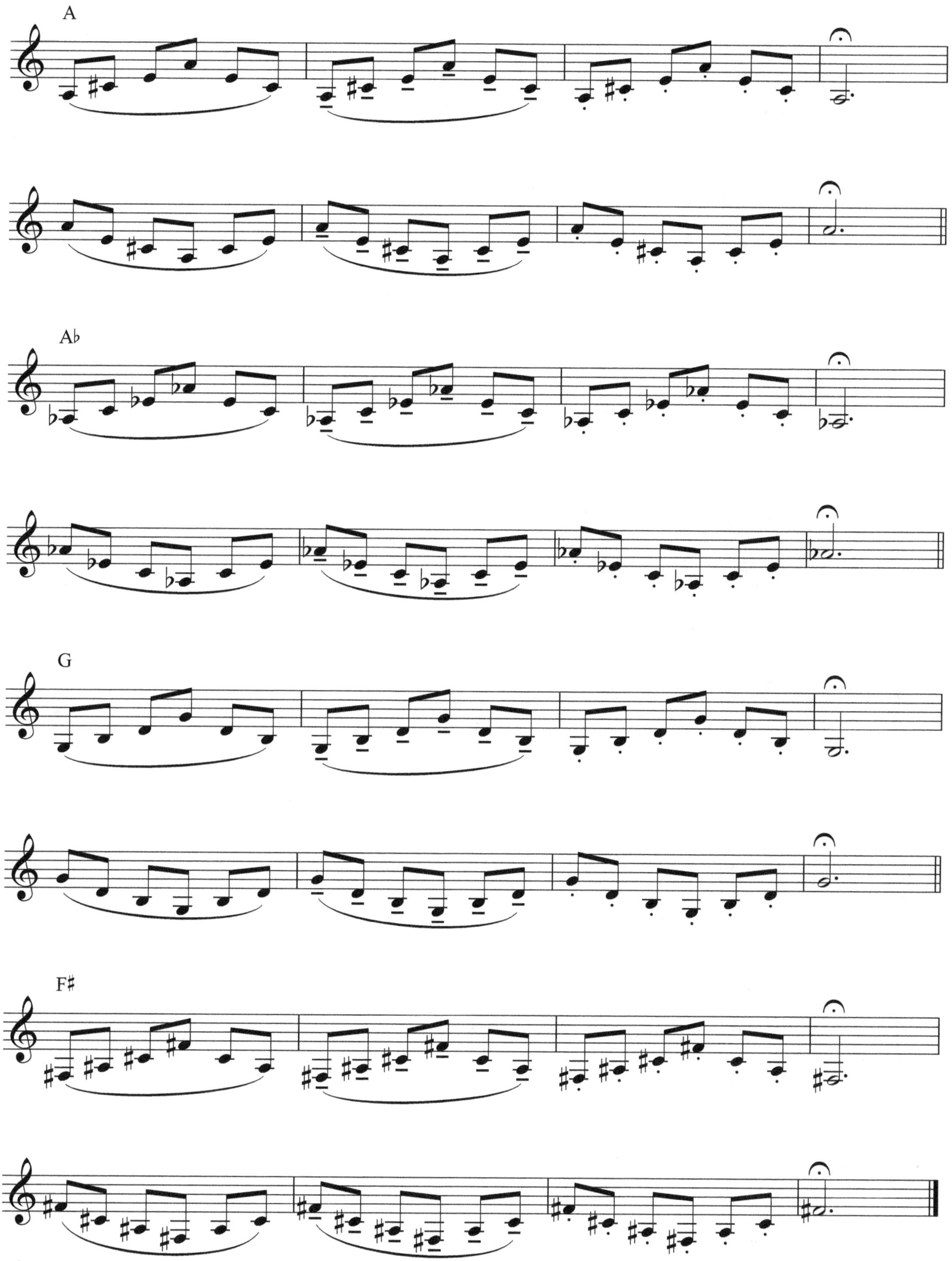
A
A♭
G
F♯

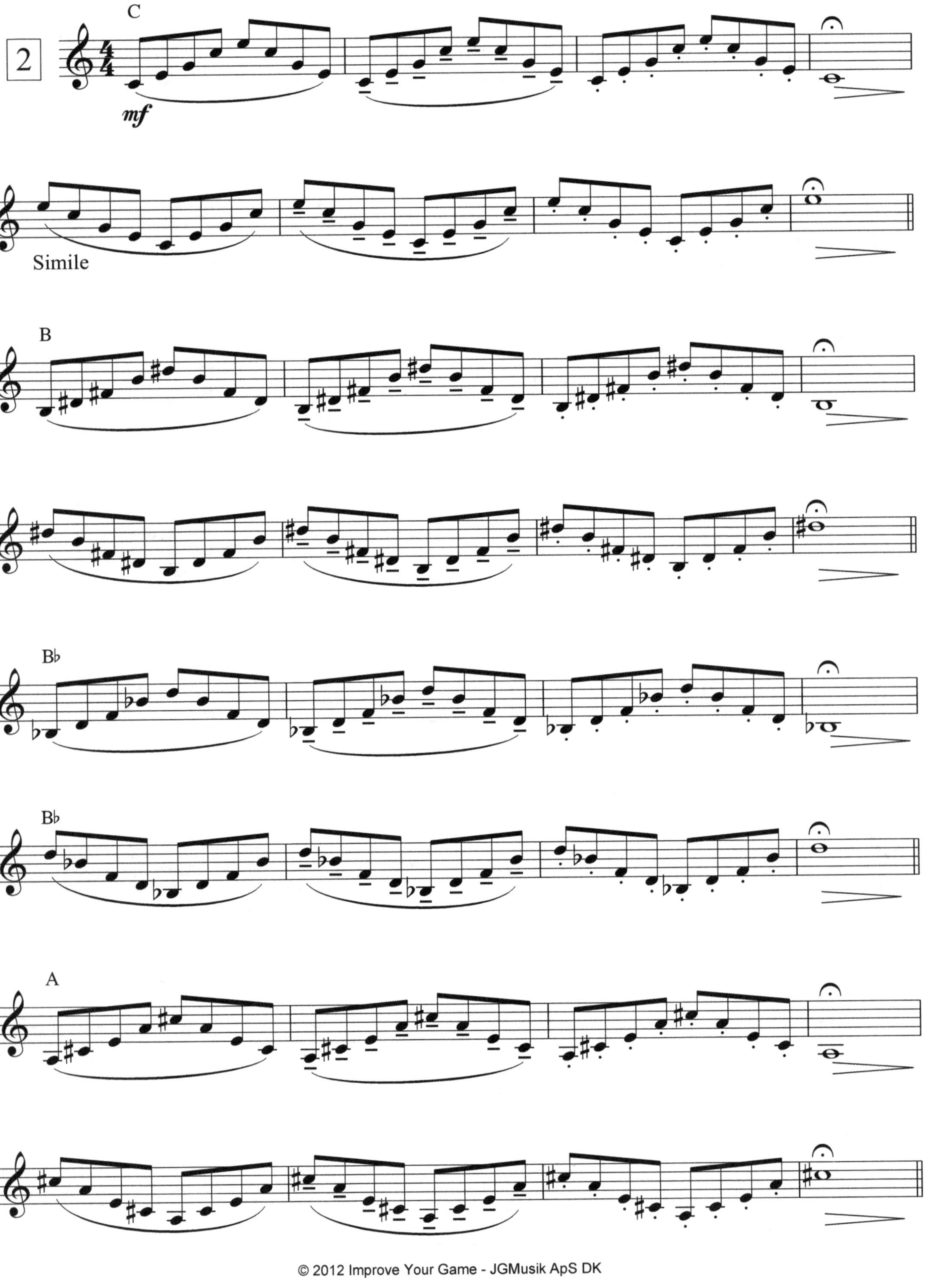
2
C
mf
Simile
B
B♭
B♭
A

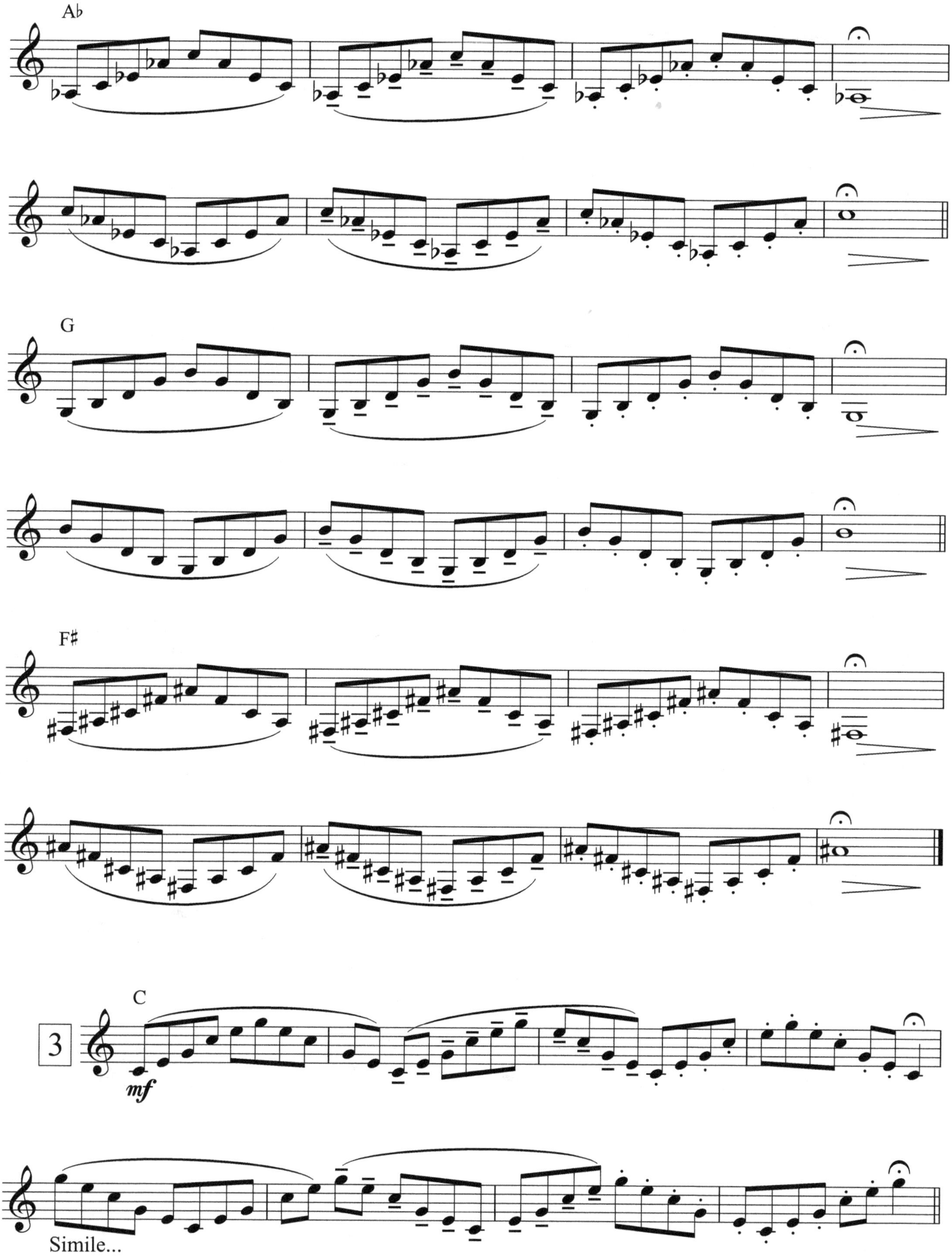
A♭
G
F♯
3
C
mf
Simile...

26

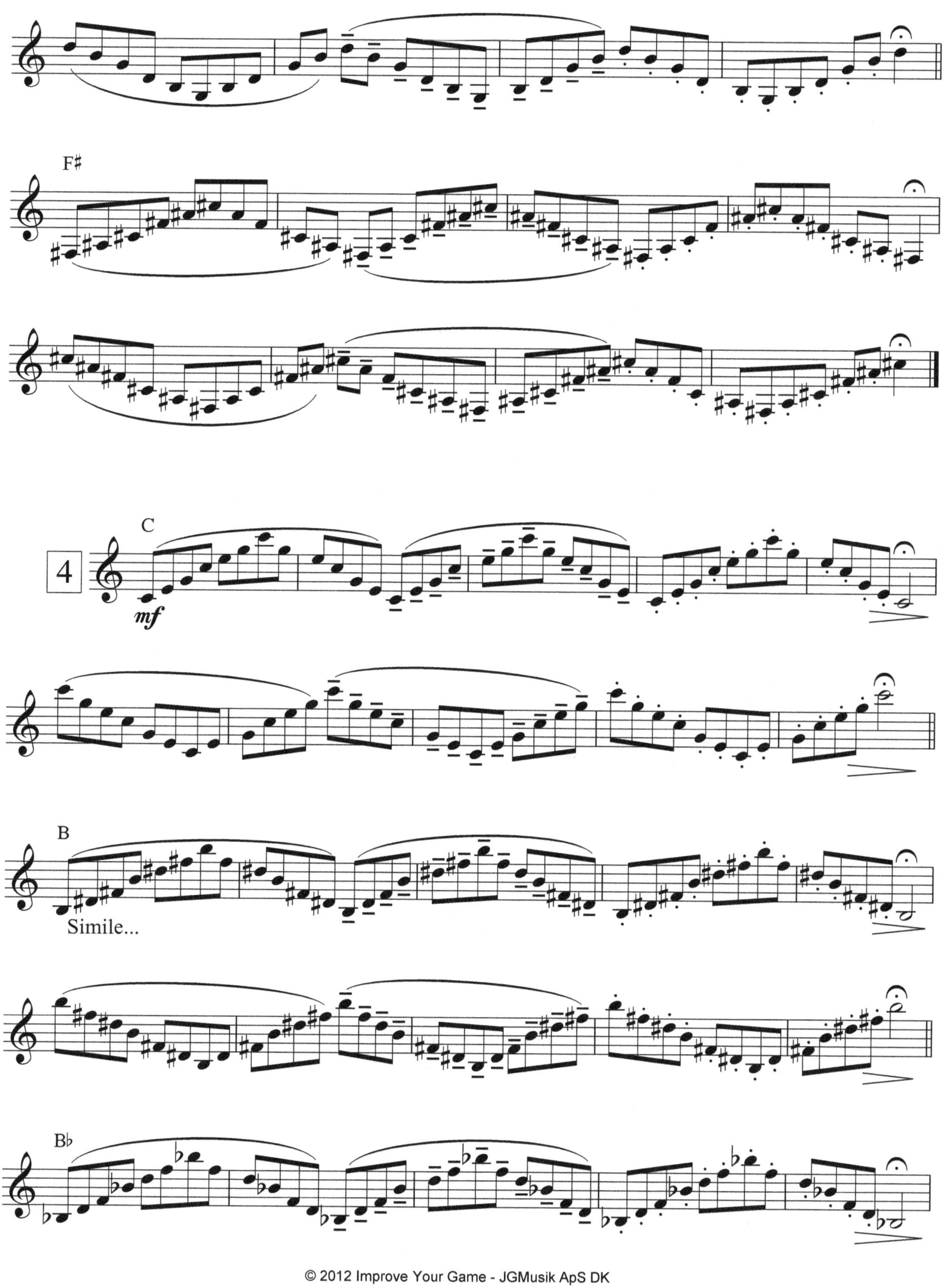
F♯
C
4
mf
B
Simile...
B♭

28

My second choice

Alternative Warm-Up

Please read "Introduction To Chapters" for reference - see index

Simile....................

Conclusion:

2 ♩ = 60

mf ——— mp ——

Simile.......................

Conclusion:

Don't read - use your brain

Interval Cadenza

Please read "Introduction To Chapters" for reference - see index

Suggestions for articulations

♩ = 100-160

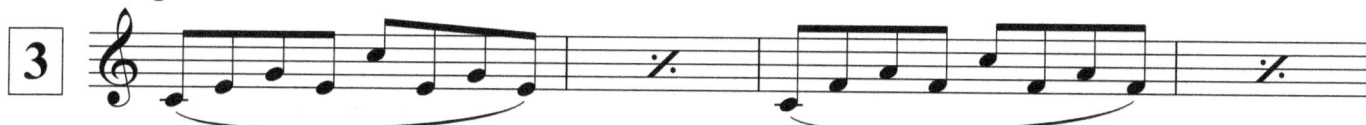

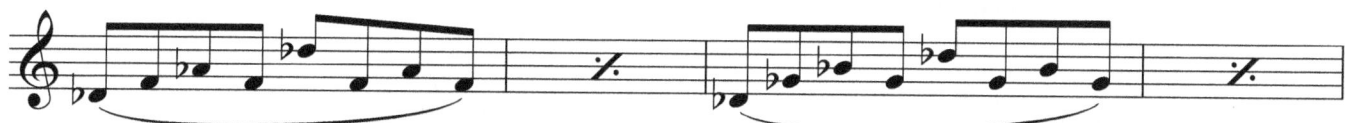

32

E

F

F#

G

Ab

A

B♭

B

C

Open up your sound

Scale-Singing

Please read "Introduction To Chapters" for reference - see index

Simile........

Simile........

Simile........

Simile........

Simile........

Simile........

Conclusion:

Take a deeeeeeep breath!

Wider Scale -"Singing"

Please read "Introduction To Chapters" for reference - see index

♩- Your Choice

repeat 2-3 x

5

Simile.......

Simile.......

Simile.......

Simile.......

Simile.......

Do not continue to Ex. #6 before mastering Ex. #5 without getting tired

Cool down phrase (*if stopping here - otherwise skip*)

Take a 10 minute break

Only play this exercise if it is within your range. Push yourself but don't force the notes!!
Three attempts per key. If the notes do not come - STOP!! It'll come tomorrow :-)
So remember: *"3 strikes and you're out!"*

Cool down phrase

Take a 10 minute break

Doesn't sound good - and it shouldn't

The Lip Bender Warm-Up

Please read "Introduction To Chapters" for reference - see index

♩ = **60** Use written fingering where indicated.

B
2...
2...
E
12...
12...
A
12...
12...
D
13...
13...
G
0.....
0.....
2
Bend w/lips
0...
2...
1...
mf
Simile......
12...
0...
2...
1...
12...
Very Hard to do
0...
2...
1...
0...

40

Be precise with the intervals

Flexibility Warm-Up

Please read "Introduction To Chapters" for reference - see index

Only if within your range - Remember: *"3 strikes and you're out!!"*

Only if within your range - Remember: "*3 strikes and you're out!!*"

After cool down phrase - take a 10 minute break before continuing

Cool down phrase

5

Only if within your range - Remember: "3 strikes and you're out!!"

After cool down phrase - take a 10 minute break before continuing

Cool down phrase

6

Only if within your range - Remember: "*3 strikes and you're out!!*"

After cool down phrase - take a 10 minute break before continuing

Cool down phrase

7 *mp*

mf

Only if within your range - Remember:"3 strikes and you're out!!"

f *ff*

8 *mp*

mf

Only if within your range - Remember:"3 strikes and you're out!!"

ff

After cool down phrase - take a 10 minute break before continuing

Cool down phrase

f 8vb

Legato Power Warm-Up

Please read "Introduction To Chapters" for reference - see index

You know the feeling. Some days it feels like someone left something inside your horn. The resistance feels crazy, but the problem is that your sound just hasn't opened up. The day after a tough gig can be one of those days. This exercise helps you open up your sound again. No key signatures - just all the "white keys" is the base of this exercise. This one is a no brainer - just focus on air and sound.

Play with an open and full sound, and think of each phrase as one long AAAAAAAHHHHHHHHHH!

Play only within your range and with the principle: "*3 strikes and you're out!!*"

46

F alternative

Simile......

Simile......

G alternative

Simile......

A alternative

Simile......

Simile......

B alternative

Simile......

C alternative

Simile......

Cooldown alternative

Simile......

Don't end your warm-up without this!!

Danish Folk Song

Please read "Introduction To Chapters" for reference - see index

Tip: Blow freely with a full sound!!

Andante Cantabile

Wait 1-2 minutes before playing next version

Andante Cantabile

Wait 1-2 minutes before playing next version

Andante Cantabile

Cool down phrase

Take 10 minute break before continuing

WISE TRUMPET TAPAS - "PRACTISING"

Get "set" before you play your first note.

When seated, be ready to stand - When standing, be ready to run.

EVERYBODY WANTS TO BE THE HERO BUT NO ONE WANTS TO SLAY THE DRAGON

WYNTON MARSALIS

Analysis is paralysis.

Know if you are a color or the lead

A section player must be selfless, willing to make the other players sound good by blending with them.

If your lyrical playing is strong, make your technical playing match it

Old habits do not disappear. New habits take the place of old. If you're lazy, old habits will take over.

Play with the most beautiful sound you can imagine

Take a day off each week – it's just trumpet playing!!

Interval Studies
Major, minor & Augmented

Please read "Introduction To Chapters" for reference - see index

Six suggestions for articulation

♩ = your choice (Remember - Nothing is so fast that it can't be played slower) :-)

Interval Studies - Major

© 2012 Improve Your Game - JGMusik ApS DK

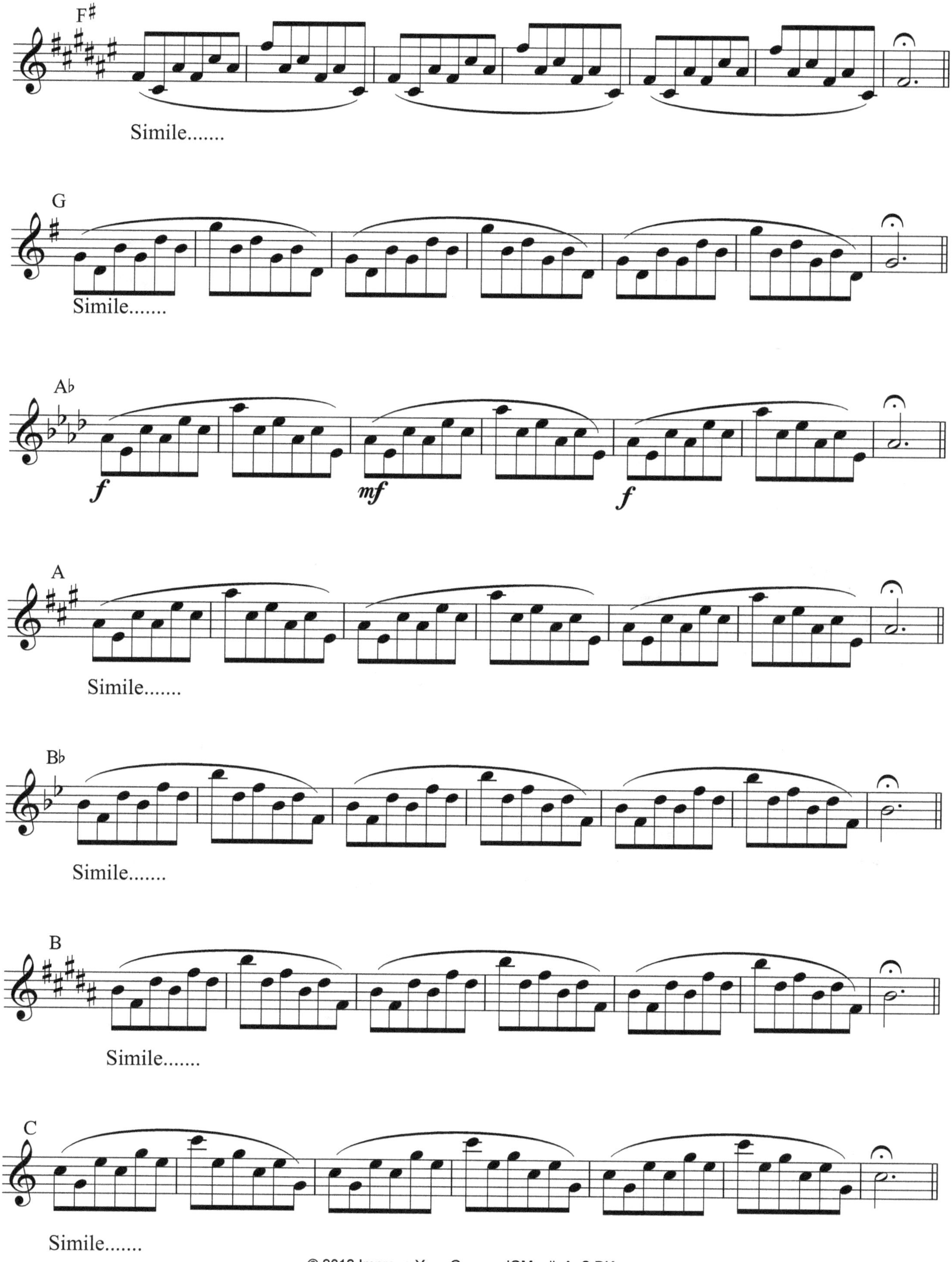
F♯
Simile.......
G
Simile.......
A♭
f
mf
f
A
Simile.......
B♭
Simile.......
B
Simile.......
C
Simile.......

Interval Studies - minor

Apply same articulations as in exercise 1

♩ = your choice

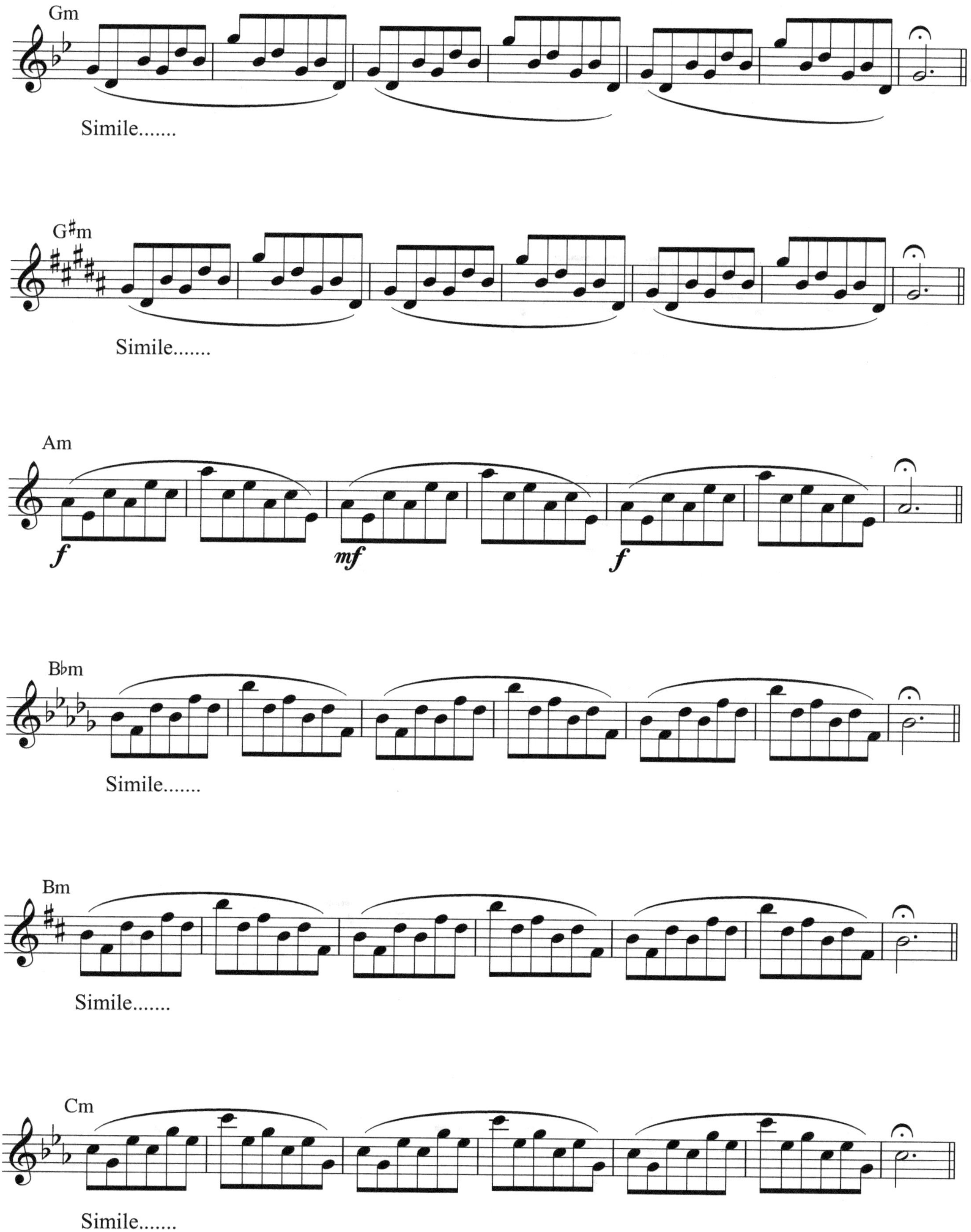
Gm
Simile.......
G♯m
Simile.......
Am
f
mf
f
B♭m
Simile.......
Bm
Simile.......
Cm
Simile.......

Interval Studies - Augmented (#5)

Apply same articulations as in exercise 1

♩ = your choice

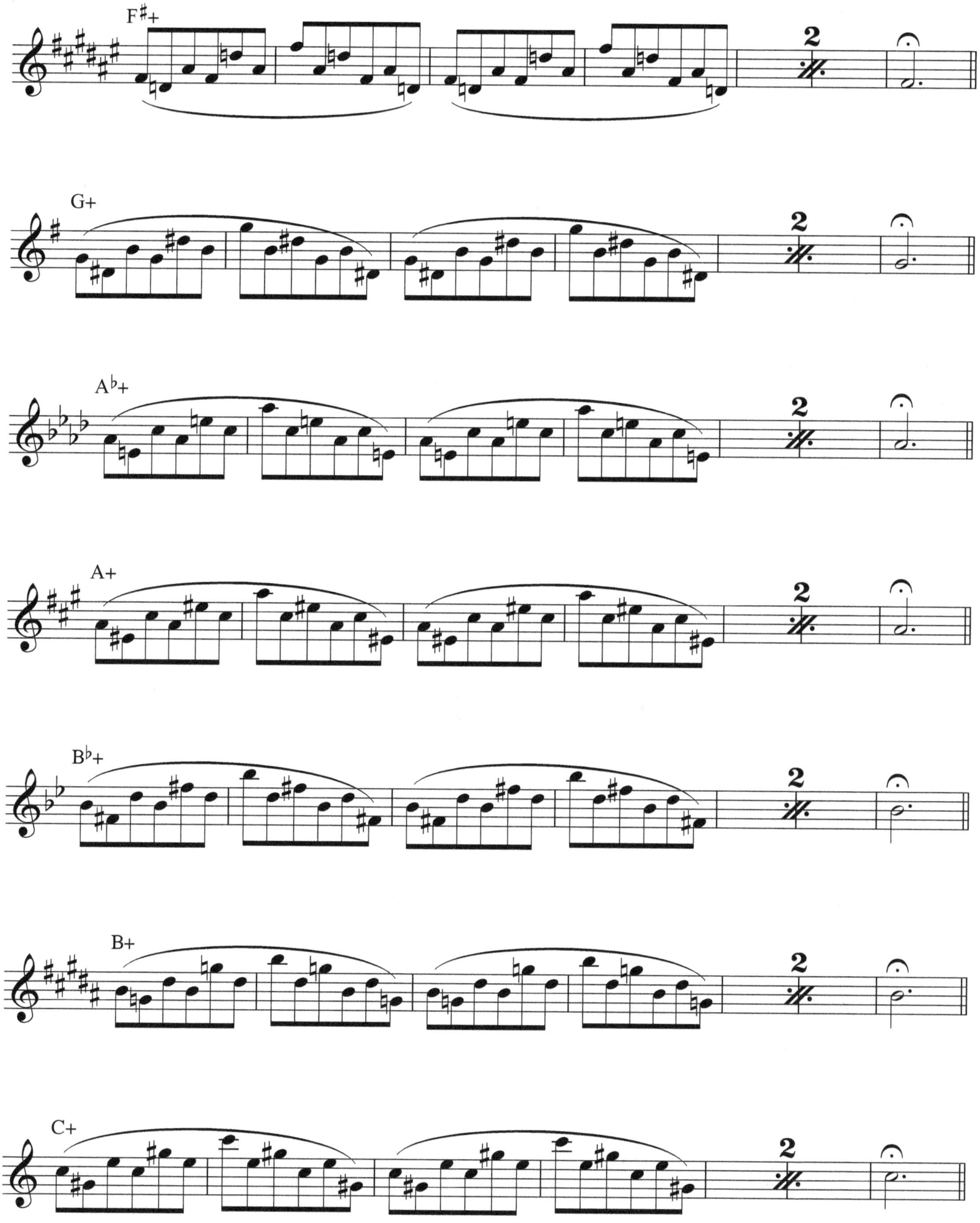
F♯+
2
G+
2
A♭+
2
A+
2
B♭+
2
B+
2
C+
2

Interval Studies - Major, minor & Augmented (#5)

Apply same articulations as in exercise 1

♩ = your choice

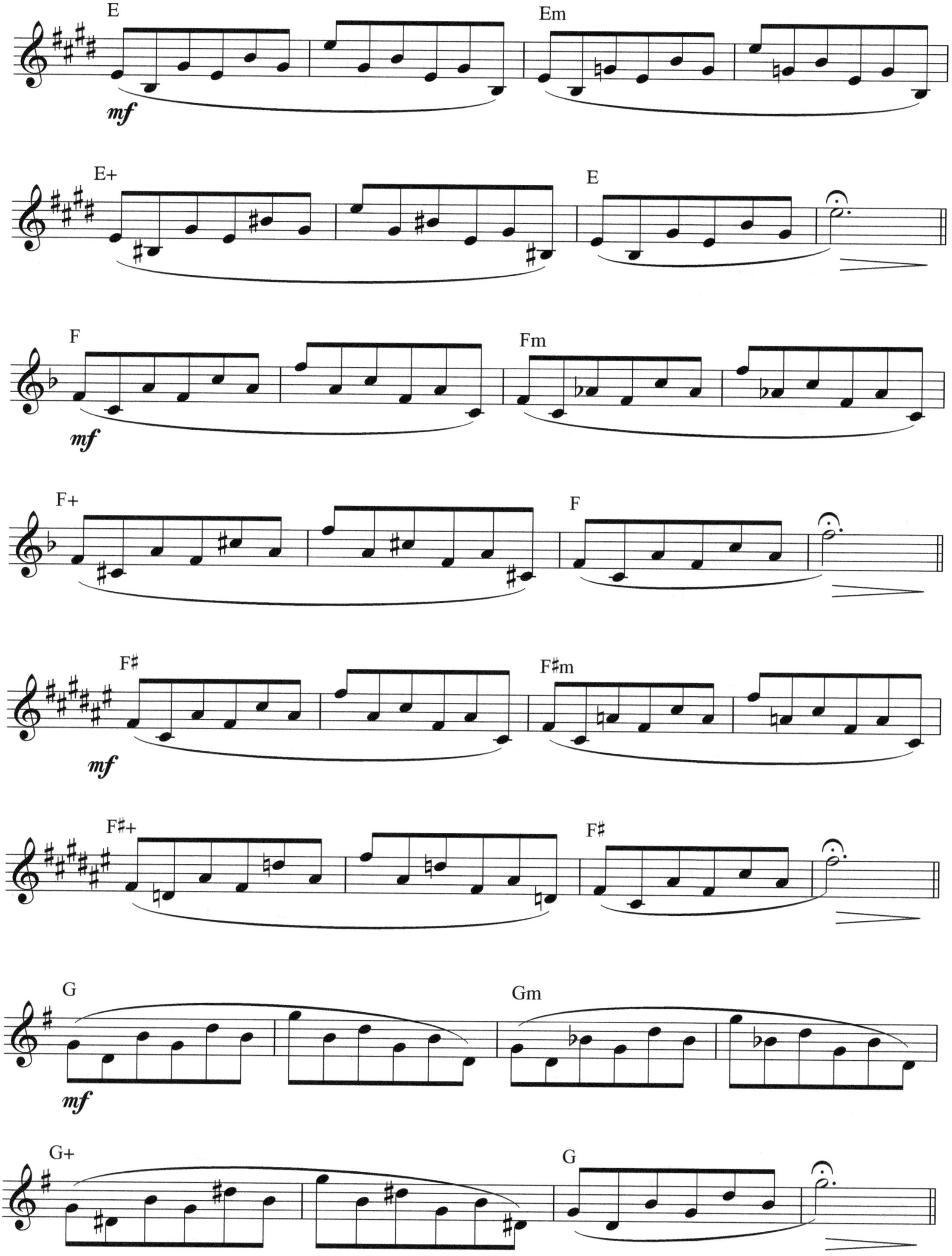
E
mf
Em
E+
E
F
mf
Fm
F+
F
F♯
mf
F♯m
F♯+
F♯
G
mf
Gm
G+
G

58

Cool down phrase

Take a 10 minute break

Boring - but rewarding

Expanding Flexibility-Slur Study - Half Notes

Please read "Introduction To Chapters" for reference - see index

Alternative articulations:

Stop here and play the cool down phrase if the rest of exercise is not within your range.

Cool down phrase

Take A Ten Minute Break

Play only if within your range. Remember - *"3 strikes and you're out"*

Simile.......

Cool down phrase

Take A Ten Minute Break

WISE TRUMPET TAPAS - "PRACTISE"

Practise pianissimo

Assign yourself material and stay with it daily for a specific number of days (6 to 10)

CONSIDER DEVOTING LESS TIME TO REPETITIVE MATERIAL, AND MORE TIME DOING MUSICAL MATERIAL

Practise playing on cold chops in order to be ready for any situation

Always incorporate music into your warm up.

Do something else to fill the space while you are resting – internet for instance:-)

Rest as much as you play.

Use pedal tones and a 10-20 min. rest to extend your practise.

Set small realistic goals for yourself – every day

Practise with a friend!!

Better slow and precise than fast and sloppy

Expanding Flexibility-Slur Study - Quarter Notes

Please read "Introduction To Chapters" for reference - see index

Alternative articulations

♩ = your choice

Simile.......

Simile.......

Stop here and play the cool down phrase if the rest of the exercise is not within your range - otherwise continue

© 2012 Improve Your Game - JGMusik ApS DK

Cool down phrase

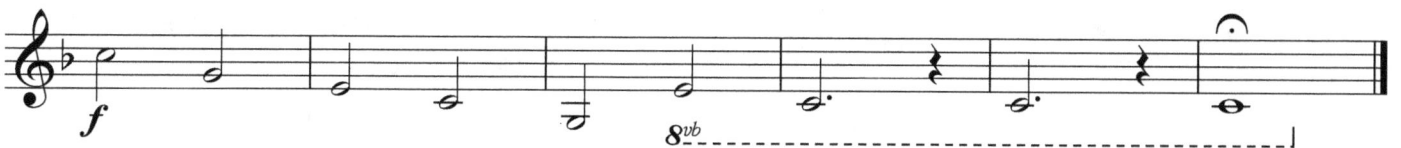

Take A Ten Minute Break

Play only if within your range

4 Db

D

Simile.......

Eb

Simile.......

E

Simile.......

F

Simile.......

After Cool Down Phrase -Take A Ten Minute Break

Cool down phrase

Again -Better slow and precise than fast and sloppy

Expanding Flexibility-Study - Eighth Notes

Please read "Introduction To Chapters" for reference - see index

Alternative articulations

Stop here and play the cool down phrase if the rest of the exercise is not within your range - otherwise continue

Cool down phrase

Take A Ten Minute Break

Play only if within your range

6 Db

D

Simile.......

Eb

Simile.......

E

Simile.......

F

Simile.......

Cool down phrase

Take A Ten Minute Break

If you think this is easy - think again!

Expanding Flexibility-Study - Sixteenth Notes

Please read "Introduction To Chapters" for reference - see index

No alternative articulations suggested

♩ = your choice

If you want to play this higher - *join the circus!* :-)

Cool down phrase

Take A Ten Minute Break

I grew up on Arban - I owe him a lot!!

Arban-inspired Slur/Flexibility Study

Please read "Introduction To Chapters" for reference - see index

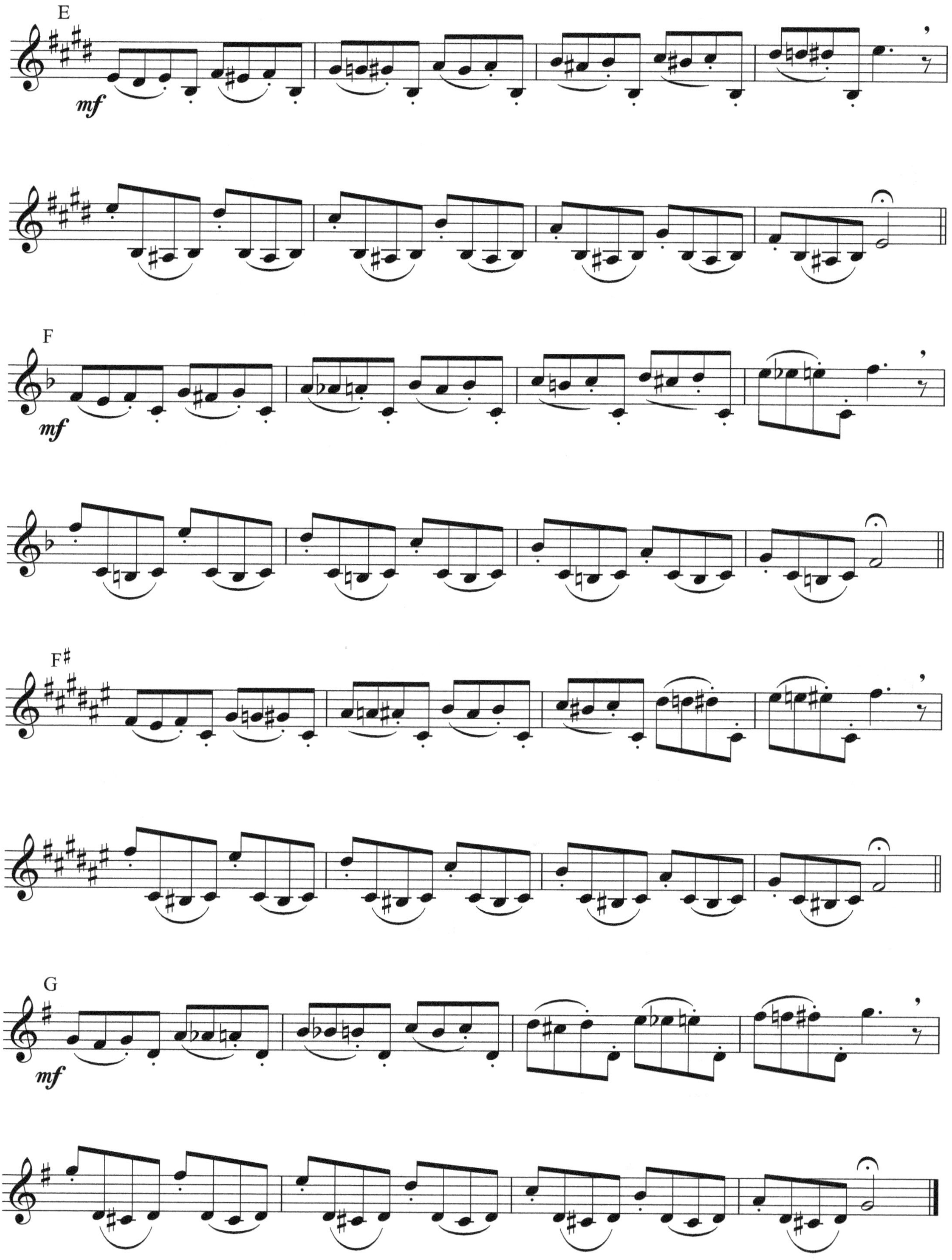
E
mf
F
mf
F♯
G
mf

72

I promise - we're done soon!!

Interval Range Study

Please read "Introduction To Chapters" for reference - see index

Alternative articulations

D

rit.

accel.

a tempo

E♭

rit.

accel.

a tempo

E

rit.

accel.

a tempo

Stop here and play cool down phrase if the rest of the exercise is not within your range

Cool down phrase

Take A Ten Minute Break

Play only if within your range

G

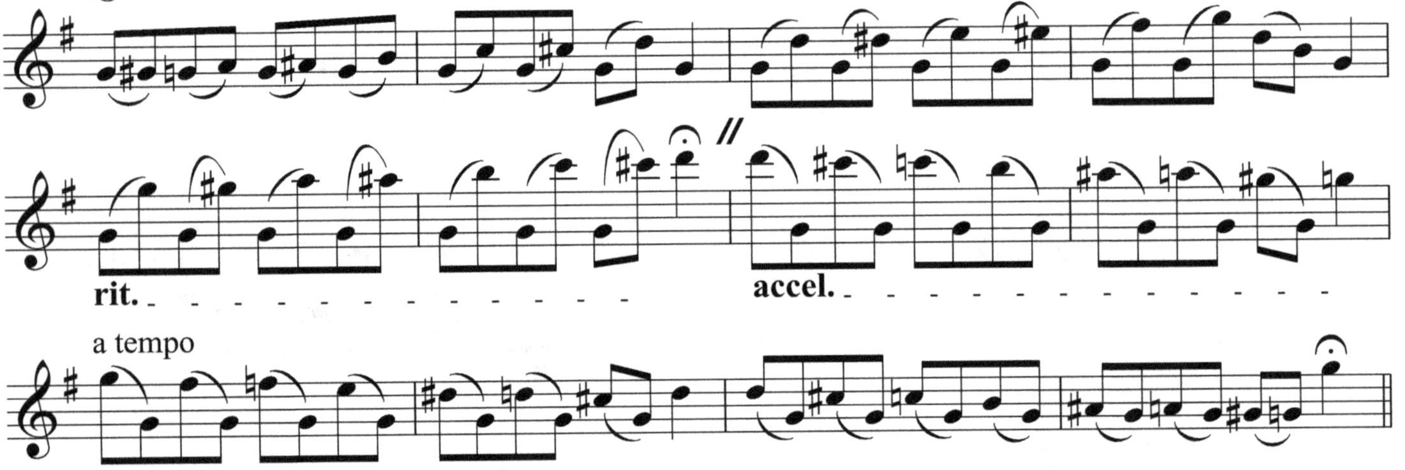

A♭

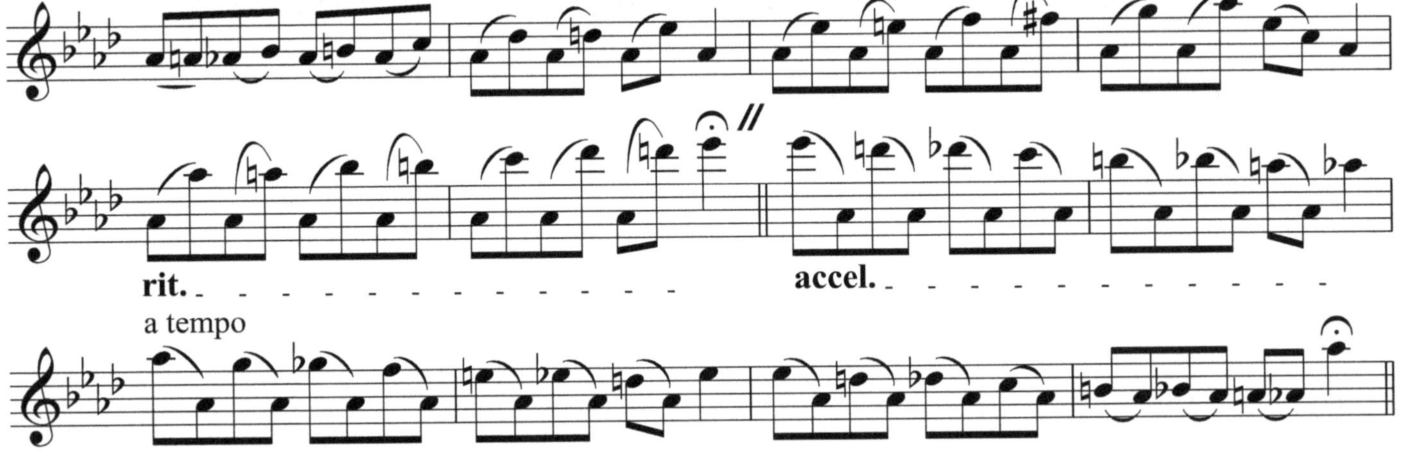

A

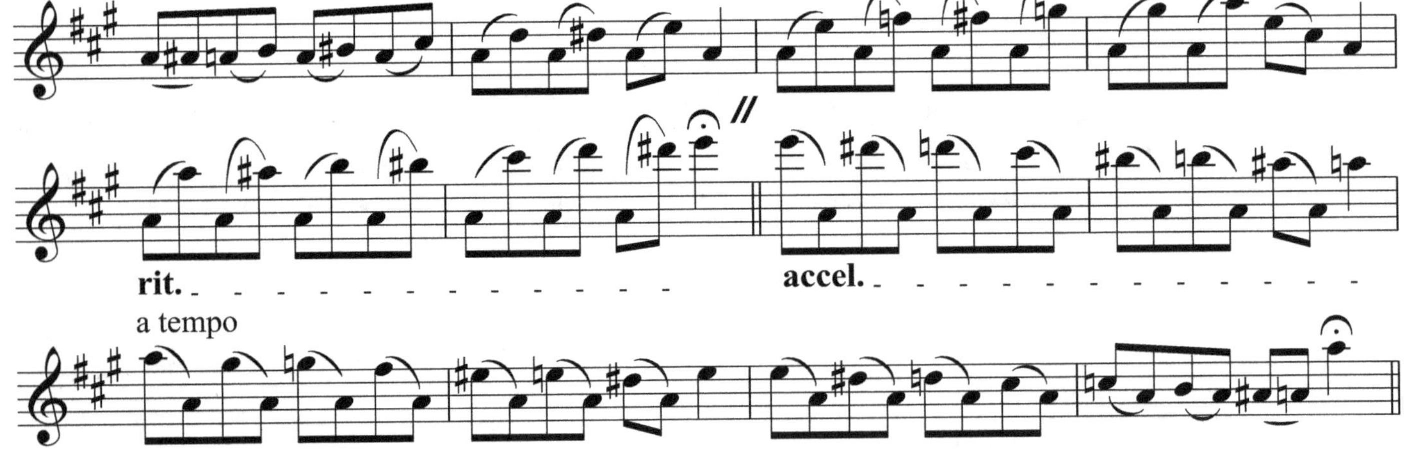

Cool down phrase

Take A Ten Minute Break

Introduction To Octave Studies

These next octave studies are extremely difficult – but necessary. There are several purposes, but the most important is to improve your accuracy. If you showed up to a gig and were presented with music with phrases like the ones you're about to play, you would say that they were not written for trumpet. Well, they are not.
BUT – if you can master them your accuracy rate will improve drastically.

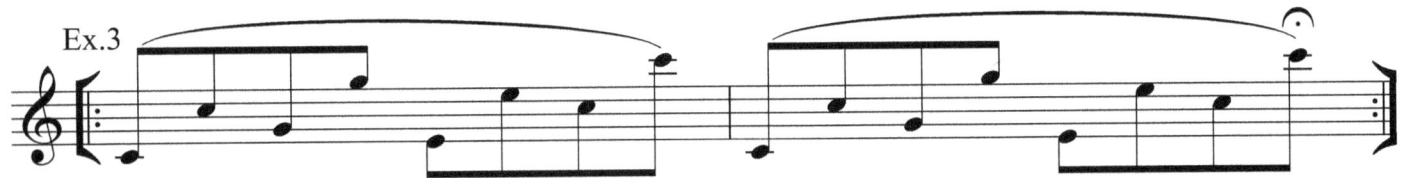

To be accurate while descending is as difficult as being accurate ascending - and just as important. Exercises 3 and 4 focus on descending. Here are a couple of tips for playing both exercises:

To avoid hitting wrong notes you often develop the bad habit of under-blowing high notes, while compensating with increased muscle tension. Forget that and back your intentions up WITH AIR. That will solve the problem and give you great confidence. Only play exercises 2 and 4 after you have mastered exercises 1 and 3.
Don't overdo it - that would be counterproductive..

Octave Studies

(Please read introduction on previous page)

(note: fermata in every second bar)

♩ = your choice

1

Simile......

80

Remember - *"3 strikes and you're out!"*

Simile......

Simile......

Remember - "*3 strikes and you're out!*"

Simile......

Octave Legato Study

(Please read introduction to chapter for reference)

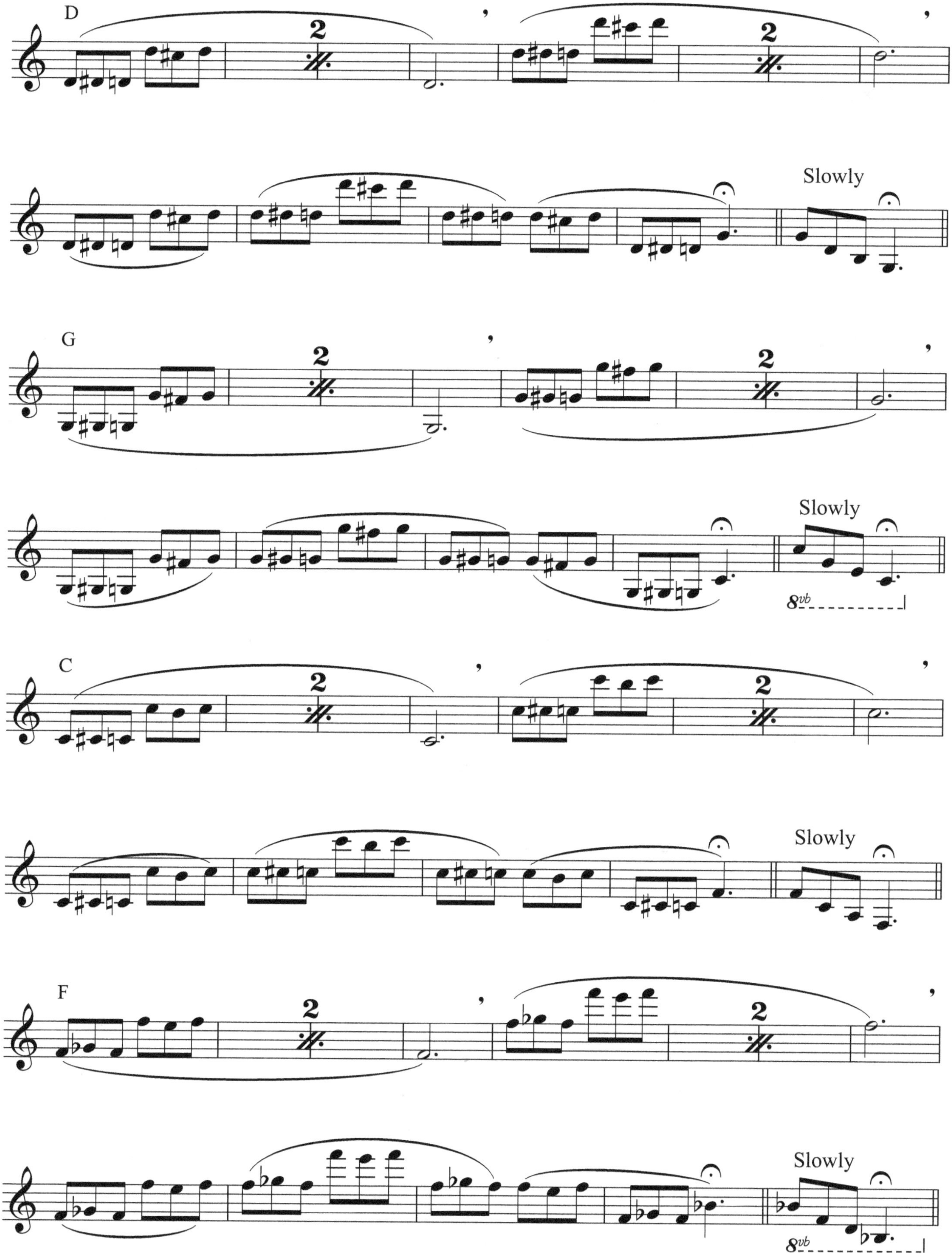
D
2
2
Slowly
G
2
2
Slowly
8vb
C
2
2
Slowly
F
2
2
Slowly
8vb

84

WISE TRUMPET TAPAS - "THE INSTRUMENT"

Don't mistake volume for intensity

SLAM THE VALVES. JUST THROW THE BALL - DON'T THINK!!

Ease mouthpiece pressure at all rests and phrase endings

Make your primary instrument the Bb trumpet. C trumpet makes you tight.

When choosing a mouthpiece, consider having somebody listen to you from across the room

Mouthpiece: The best solutions come from retaining the cup, throat and changing the rim and changing the backbore.

Do not owerblow!!

ON C TRUMPET, ALWAYS USE 23 FOR EB AND 12 FOR E - DO NOT USE 13 FOR D OR HIGH G

Practise piccolo parts on Bb trumpet.

Know when to use alternate fingerings and when they are not needed.

Sing!

Finally - some real music - thank you!!

Lyrical Etudes - Level 1

Jan Glaesel

Jan Glaesel

Jan Glaesel

Jan Glaesel

Presto con brio

Rubato　　　a tempo

Animato Caprissioso

Jan Glaesel

Jan Glaesel

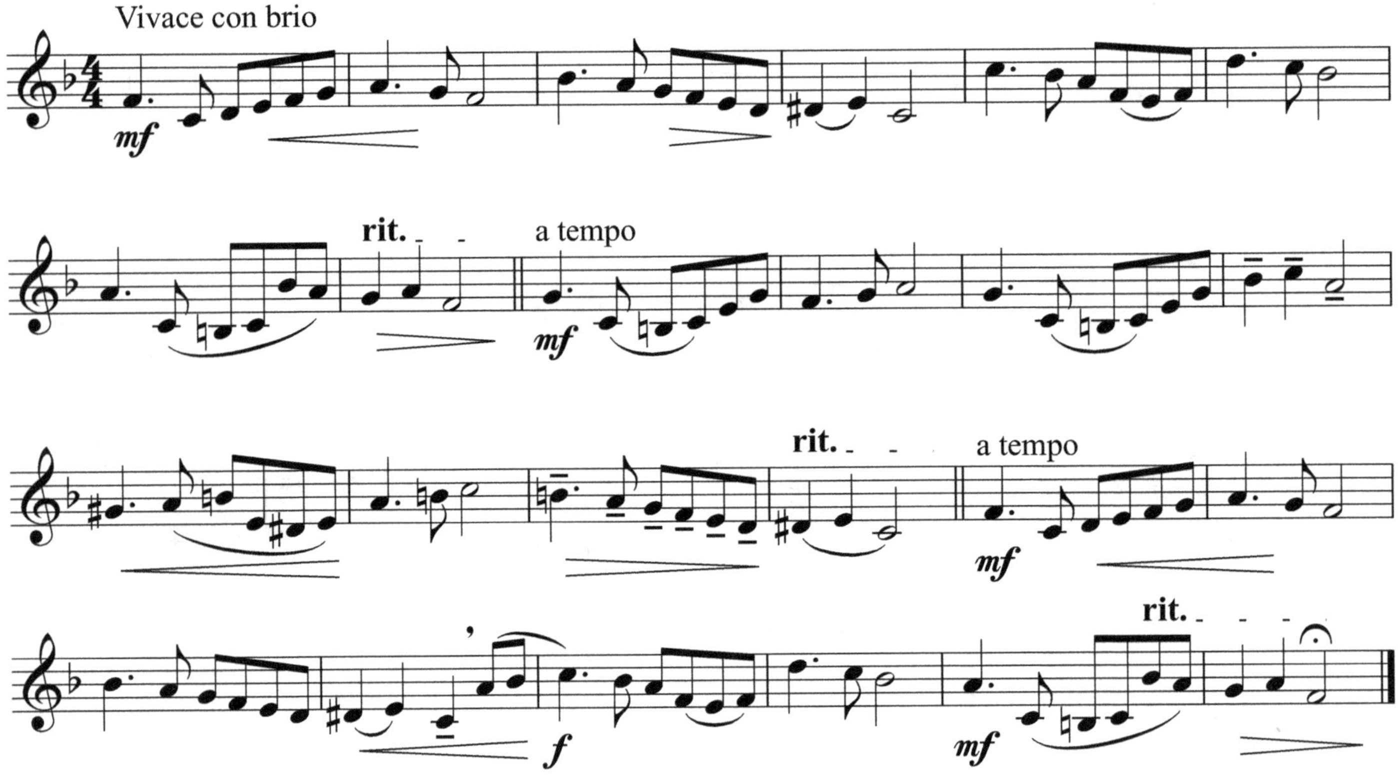

WISE TRUMPET TAPAS - "BREATHING"

Do not owerblow!!

DON'T FORCE THE AIR

DON'T HOLD BACK THE AIR.

Use the nosebreath to avoid unseating the embouchure

Accelerate the air when ascending - decelerate the air when descending.

It's important to blow freely, so as not to crush the lips and pinch the tone

Breathe as though you were going to swim underwater to the other side of the pool.

Use slow breathing - in through the nose and out through the mouth - to counteract performance anxiety.

Breathe up until the point of playing.

On a scale from 1-10, take a "10" breath every time

Fill your lungs from the bottom and use them as a bellows

Blow through the notes

Trumpet Menuet Etude - D minor

Jan Glaesel

Allegretto Animato

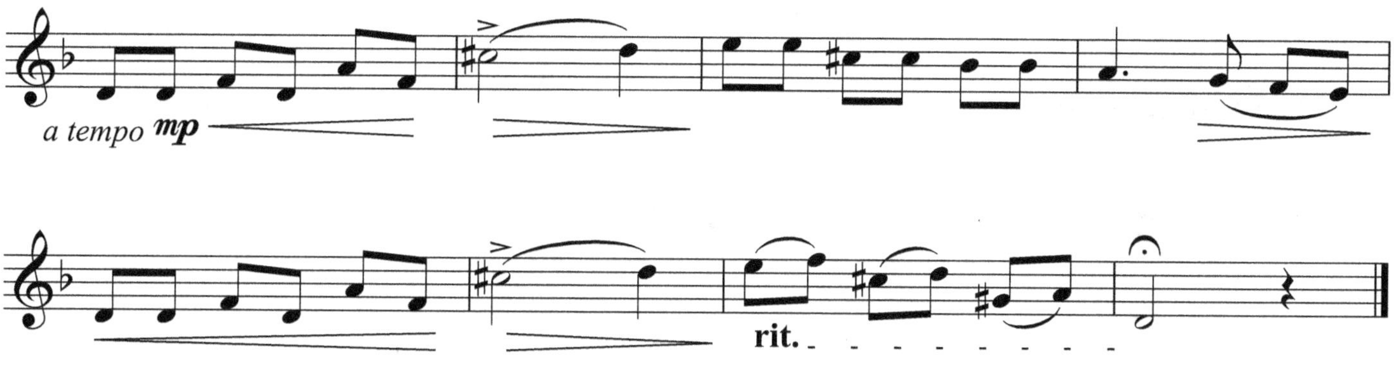
a tempo
mp
rit.

Dedicated to trumpetplayer Per Nielsen

Etude Melancolico

Jan Glæsel

Largo con russa expressivo

poco rit. _ _ _ _ _ _ _

Atempo

poco rit. _ _ _ _ _ _ _

Meno mosso

poco rit. _ _ _ _ _ _ _

Andante Cantabile ♩ = 88

mf

Agitato   rit. _ _ _ _   *Rubato*

ff   *p*

Rubato

p —— *mp* —— *mf* ——

Largo expressivo

Atempo *mp*

Agitato   rit. _ _ _ _ _ _ _

mf —— *f*   *mp*

Dedicated to Malcolm McNab - trumpet virtuoso L.A.

Lyrical interval Etude

Jan Glaesel

molto rit.

pp

tempo 1

mp   *f*   *mp*   *f*

p   *mf*

mp   *mf*   *mp*   *mf*

accel. _ _ _ _ _   rit. _ _ _   accel. _ _ _ _ _   rit. _ _

pp

accel. _ _ _ _ _ _ _   rit. _ _ _

MY BOOKSHELF OF CONSTANT INSPIRATION

When I started to practice for real in 2004 the only method-book I had was:

J.S. ARBAN - COMPLETE CONSERVATORY METHOD FOR TRUMPET

This was the book I was handed back in 1967 when I join the Tivoli Boys Guard here in Copenhagen. I think it is considered one of the "bibles" for many trumpet players. In 2004 when I began my new journey I started collecting all kinds of trumpet method books. Here is a list of the content of "My bookshelf of constant inspiration", in random order.

Author	Title	Publisher
J.B. Arban	Complete Conservatory Method for Trumpet	Carl Fischer
Herbert L. Clarke	Technical Studies for the Cornet	Carl Fischer
Arturo Sandoval	Playing techniques & Performance Studies Vol. 1-3	Hal Leonard
James Stamp	Warm-Ups & Studies	Editions BIM
Claude Gordon	Systematic Approach to Daily Practice	Carl Fischer
Allen Vizzutti	The Allen Vizzutti Trumpet Method Vol. 1-3	Alfred Publishing
Geoff Winstead	The Real Way to Play the Cat Anderson Method	GWM Publishing
Carmine Caruso	Musical Calisthenics for Brass	Hal Leonard
Max Schlossberg	Daily Drills & Technical Studies for Trumpet	M. Baron Company
Gabriel Parés Parés	Scales for Cornet or Trumpet	Rubank - Hal Leonard
J.L. Small	27 Melodious and Rhythmical Exercises	Carl Fischer
David Vining	Ear training for Trumpet	Carl Fischer
John McNeil	Jazz Trumpet Techniques	Studio P/R
Charles Colin	Advanced Lip Flexibilities Vol. 1-3	Charles Colin Music
Charles Colin	Complete Modern Method for Trumpet or Cornet	Charles Colin Music
Jon Gorrie	High notes, Low Notes and Everything in Between	www.jongorrie.com

I've worked with all of these books and found, through them, inspiration for my own approach to trumpet playing. I pay my deepest respects to all of the writers, and it's with the utmost humility I've used them as inspiration for my version of the ultimate Trumpet Method Book.

MUSICAL STUDIES & ETUDES:

Musical studies and etudes are just as important as technical studies. Below you will find some of my favorite collections from my bookshelf. I divide my time between Technical Studies, Musical Studies and Etudes 50/50 - I urge you to do the same.

Author	Title	Publisher
Sigmund Hering	Thirty Etudes for Trumpet or Cornet	Carl Fischer
Sigmund Hering	Thirty-two Etudes for Trumpet or Cornet	Carl Fischer
Sigmund Hering	Forty Progressive Etudes for Trumpet	Carl Fischer
Kopprasch	Sixty Selected Studies for Trumpet	Carl Fischer
H. Voxman	H. Selected Studies for Cornet or Trumpet	Rubank - Hal Leonard
H. Voxman	H. Selected Duets for Cornet or Trumpet Vol. 1-2	Rubank - Hal Leonard
H. Voxman	Concert&Contest Collection for Cornet or Trumpet	Rubank - Hal Leonard
Larry Clark	Progressive Duets for Trumpet in Bb Vol. 1-2	Carl Fischer
Walter Beeler	Solos for the Trumpet-Player	G. Schirmer - Hal Leonard

CREDITS:

Most of all I want, I want thank my loving wife Miriam and the rest of my family for enduring the "awful" sound of practising the trumpet - Thanks guys!!

A special thanks goes to my good friend, and fellow trumpet player **Gary Cordell,** Las Vegas Nevada, for proofreading this project. Also thank you for introducing me to Tony Scodwell.

Tony Scodwell - my good friend and fellow trumpet player, for letting me play one of his fantastic handmade trumpets. "Tony - you're a true artist and craftsman building your fantastic horns."

Bob Reeves - mouthpieces. Thank you for taking almost a day out of your busy schedule to guide me to the mouthpieces which are going to follow me, for the rest of my life.

Jon Gorrie - for opening my eyes to the Print On Demand concept. Also for helping me setting up the whole online marketing side of the project - Let's do something more together.

Krogstrup & Hede - web bureau. For always doing your best for my websites.

Bithiah & Patrick Poulsen - Layout. I love the cover and all your input - thank you.

The Danish Musical Directors Union - for financial support.

Please feel free to contact me with feedback or questions at info@trumpetgame.com

www.ingramcontent.com/pod-product-compliance
Lightning Source LLC
Chambersburg PA
CBHW081634040426
42449CB00014B/3306